THE GRAPHIC SHAKESPEARE SERIES

A MIDSUMMER NIGHT'S DREAM

RETOLD BY HILARY BURNINGHAM
ILLUSTRATED BY ZARA SLATTERY

EVANS BROTHERS LIMITED

THE CHARACTERS IN THE PLAY

Theseus — Duke of Athens

Hippolyta — Queen of the Amazons, to marry Theseus

Egeus — father of Hermia

Hermia — Egeus's daughter, in love with Lysander

Lysander — in love with Hermia

Demetrius — wanted to marry Hermia

Helena — in love with Demetrius

Oberon — King of the Fairies

Titania — Queen of the Fairies

Puck, or Robin Goodfellow — servant of Oberon

Peter Quince — a carpenter; the Director of *Pyramus and Thisbe*

Nick Bottom — a weaver; Pyramus in *Pyramus and Thisbe*

Francis Flute — A bellows-mender; Thisbe in *Pyramus and Thisbe*

Tom Snout — a tinker; Wall in *Pyramus and Thisbe*

Snug — a joiner; Lion in *Pyramus and Thisbe*

Robin Starveling — a tailor; Moonshine in *Pyramus and Thisbe*

Peaseblossom }
Cobweb } fairies
Moth } servants of Titania
Mustardseed }

THE GRAPHIC
SHAKESPEARE SERIES

A MIDSUMMER NIGHT'S DREAM

Published by
Evans Brothers Limited
2A Portman Mansions
Chiltern Street
London W1U 6NR

Designed by Design Systems Ltd.

Reprinted 2007

British Library Cataloguing in Publication Data.
Burningham, Hilary
  A Midsummer Night's Dream – (The graphic Shakespeare series)
  1. Children's plays, English
  I. Title II. Slattery, Zara III. Shakespeare, William 1564-1616
  822.3'3

ISBN 978 0 237 52440 1

Printed in China by WKT Co Ltd

PORTRAIT GALLERY

Oberon

Hippolyta

Theseus

Titania

Lysander

Hermia

Demetrius

Helena

Egeus

Puck

Bottom

Quince

Flute

Starveling

Snout

Snug

ACT 1

Theseus, Duke of Athens, was to marry Hippolyta, Queen of the Amazons[1]. Theseus and his army had fought with the Amazons and beaten them. Theseus fell in love with the beautiful Hippolyta.

They were to be married in four days' time. Theseus was very happy. He wanted everyone to be happy and enjoy his wedding.

[1] Amazons - a race of female warriors

THESEUS: Hippolyta, I wooed thee with my sword,
And won thy love doing thee injuries;
But I will wed thee in another key:
With pomp, with triumph and with revelling.

Egeus came to talk to the Duke about his daughter, Hermia. He was very angry with her.

He wanted Hermia to marry Demetrius, a young nobleman.

Hermia didn't want to marry Demetrius. She was in love with Lysander.

It was the law of Athens that Hermia should do as her father wished. If not, one of two things could happen to her: she could be put to death, or she could be forced to live in a nunnery[1] for the rest of her life.

Theseus told Hermia to obey her father. That was the law.

[1] nunnery - a place where women spend their lives worshipping God

HERMIA: But I beseech your grace that I may know
         The worst that may befall me in this case
         If I refuse to wed Demetrius.
THESEUS: Either to die the death, or to abjure
         For ever the society of men.

Lysander loved Hermia and wanted to marry her. Lysander had a plan.

He asked Hermia to go away with him. They could be married. They would be far away from the law of Athens. Hermia would not be put to death or sent to a nunnery.

He asked Hermia to meet him in the woods the next night. She agreed.

LYSANDER: There, gentle Hermia, may I marry thee;
And to that place the sharp Athenian law
Cannot pursue us.

Hermia's friend, Helena, loved Demetrius. She was very unhappy because Demetrius wanted to marry Hermia. Demetrius had loved Helena first.

Hermia and Lysander told Helena that they were planning to go away together. With Hermia out of the way, perhaps Demetrius would love Helena.

When she was alone, Helena remembered how Demetrius used to love her. If she told Demetrius that Hermia was going away with Lysander, he might follow them to the woods. Perhaps he would thank Helena for telling him. He might even love her again.

HELENA: I will go tell him of fair Hermia's flight.
Then to the wood will he tomorrow night
Pursue her; and for this intelligence
If I have thanks it is a dear expense.

In another part of Athens, a group of tradesmen[1] were practising a play. They were hoping to put on their play for the Duke, Theseus, and his bride, Hippolyta, on their wedding day.

The title of the play was *Pyramus and Thisbe*. The leader of the group was Peter Quince. Peter Quince was telling the actors which part they would play. Bottom kept interrupting him. He tried to tell everyone what to do. He thought he could play all the parts better than anyone else.

[1] tradesmen - people who have a particular skill, such as woodworking, or mending things

BOTTOM: What is Pyramus? – a lover or a tyrant?
QUINCE: A lover that kills himself, most gallant, for love.
BOTTOM: That will ask some tears in the true performing of it. If I do it, let the audience look to their eyes! I will move storms. I will condole in some measure.

Peter Quince said that Flute should take the part of Thisbe, the lady that Pyramus loved. Flute didn't want to take the part of a woman[1] because he was beginning to have a beard.

Of course, Bottom thought that he could be Thisbe. He pretended to speak in a high, squeaky voice.

Snug, the joiner[2], was to take the part of the lion. He didn't have a part to learn. All he had to do was roar.

Bottom thought that he would like to be the lion, and roar for all the people.

[1] In Shakespeare's time, all women's parts were played by young boys
[2] joiner - someone who does woodwork; similar to a carpenter

FLUTE: Nay, faith, let not me play a woman – I have a beard coming.

Peter Quince gave out the parts, and the lines[1] that people had to speak. They were all supposed to learn their lines, ready for the next rehearsal.

The next rehearsal was to take place on the following night in the wood outside the town.

Lysander and Hermia were meeting in the wood. Helena planned to tell Demetrius about them. Now the tradesmen planned to have their rehearsal in the wood.

A lot of things were about to happen in the wood.

[1] lines - the words in the play spoken by each person

QUINCE: But, masters, here are your parts, and I am to
entreat you, request you, and desire you to con
them by tomorrow night, and meet me in the
palace wood a mile without the town by moonlight.
There will we rehearse…

ACT 2

Puck met a fairy in the wood. The fairy served[1] Titania, the Queen of the Fairies. Puck served Oberon, the King of the Fairies.

The King and Queen of the Fairies were having a terrible quarrel. The Queen had taken a young Indian boy to be her attendant. Oberon also wanted the boy. The Queen refused to give him up. Every time the King and Queen met, they were rude to each other and said angry words. Their fairies were frightened and crept away to hide.

The fairy recognised Puck and called him by his other name, Robin Goodfellow. Puck enjoyed making mischief for everyone. He brought bad luck to some people and good luck to others. He made Oberon laugh.

Oberon, King of the Fairies, and Titania, Queen of the Fairies were coming. The fairy was frightened. What would happen this time?

[1] served - worked for

PUCK: The King doth keep his revels here tonight.
Take heed the Queen come not within his sight,
For Oberon is passing fell and wrath
Because that she as her attendant hath
A lovely boy stolen from an Indian king.

Oberon and Titania met, and straightaway began to quarrel. Titania told Oberon that she knew he was in love with Hippolyta. Oberon said that Titania was in love with Theseus.

Because the King and Queen of the Fairies were quarrelling, many things were going wrong for the people. The seasons were getting mixed up. The weather was very bad.

Again, Oberon asked Titania to let him have the Indian boy. Titania said that the boy's mother had been her friend. Titania said she would keep the boy and bring him up.

Titania left, before they quarrelled even more.

OBERON: Ill met by moonlight, proud Titania!
TITANIA: What, jealous Oberon? Fairy, skip hence.
          I have forsworn his bed and company.

Oberon had a plan to get even with Titania and perhaps make her change her mind about the Indian boy.

In a far away place grew a small purple flower. The juice of the flower was magic. If it was put on the eyelids of a sleeping person, that person would fall madly in love with the first person or creature he or she saw on waking.

Oberon told Puck where to find the flower and sent him to fetch it. He told Puck to be very quick.

Oberon would put the juice on Titania's eyes while she slept. When Titania awoke, she would fall in love with the first thing she saw. It might be a lion, a bear, or a wolf.

OBERON: Fetch me this herb, and be thou here again
         Ere the leviathan can swim a league.
PUCK: I'll put a girdle round about the earth
         In forty minutes!

Oberon waited for Puck to come back with the magic flower.

Demetrius came to the wood to find Lysander and Hermia. He met Helena. He was trying to run away from her.

Oberon made himself invisible and listened to them.

Helena was telling Demetrius how much she loved him. She would always love him and follow him. Demetrius told her he did not love her. He would never love her. He loved Hermia.

Demetrius went into the wood, still looking for Hermia. Helena followed him. She would never give up.

Oberon felt sorry for Helena. He thought about his magic flower. Perhaps he could use the magic flower to make Demetrius love Helena.

DEMETRIUS: Do I entice you? Do I speak you fair?
Or rather do I not in plainest truth
Tell you I do not nor I cannot love you?
HELENA: And even for that do I love you the more.
I am your spaniel; and, Demetrius,
The more you beat me I will fawn on you.

Puck returned. He had the magic flower.

Oberon knew where Titania slept. He couldn't wait to squeeze the juice of the magic flower on to her eyelids. She would wake up and fall in love with the first creature that she saw.

Oberon wanted to help Helena. He told Puck to look for a young man wearing Athenian clothes. Puck was to use the magic juice on his eyes. Oberon thought the young man would be Demetrius, who would fall in love with the first woman he saw. Oberon thought Demetrius would fall in love with Helena.

Oberon didn't know that Demetrius and Helena were not the only young people from Athens in the forest that night. Hermia and Lysander had also planned to meet in the forest.

OBERON: Hast thou the flower there? Welcome, wanderer.
PUCK: Ay, there it is.
OBERON: I pray thee give it me.

Titania's fairies had sung her to sleep. She was lying on a grassy slope among the wild flowers. The fairies had woven charms[1] around her, to keep her safe.

The charms could not keep Oberon away. He squeezed the juice of the magic flower on to Titania's eyelids. He hoped that she would wake up when some horrible creature was near. She would fall in love with the horrible creature.

[1] charms - magic words

OBERON: What thou seest when thou dost wake,
Do it for thy true love take;
Love and languish for his sake.....
Wake when some vile thing is near!

Hermia and Lysander had been wandering in the forest. It was getting dark, and they had lost their way. They were very tired.

They decided to sleep for a while until daylight. They lay down, a little way apart.

Puck looked all through the forest for the young man Oberon had told him to find. He saw Lysander lying sleeping. Here was a young man wearing Athenian clothes, and a young lady sleeping nearby. This must be the person. He squeezed the juice on Lysander's eyelids.

It was time for Puck to go back to Oberon. He was sure he had used the magic juice on the right person.

PUCK: Pretty soul, she durst not lie
        Near this lack-love, this kill-courtesy.
        Churl, upon thy eyes I thro
        All the power this charm doth owe.

Helena was still chasing Demetrius through the forest!
They passed Lysander and Hermia who were asleep.
Helena was getting tired. Demetrius ran away, leaving
her alone.

Helena stopped to rest, and saw Lysander lying on
the ground. He was lying very still. She was afraid he
might be dead. She called to him, to see if he was
awake.

He awoke. Helena was the first person he saw. He
fell madly in love with her.

Helena could not understand why Lysander had
changed so suddenly. When he told her he loved her,
she thought that he was joking. She was sure that he
still loved Hermia. She ran away into the forest, still
looking for Demetrius. Lysander followed her. The
magic juice had worked.

HELENA: But who is here? – Lysander on the ground?
            Dead – or asleep? I see no blood, no wound.
            Lysander, if you live, good sir, awake!
LYSANDER: (wakes)
            And run through fire I will for thy sweet sake!

Hermia was having bad dreams. She called out for Lysander. He would comfort her.

Lysander was nowhere to be seen. Hermia called his name again. Suddenly, she was very, very frightened. Rather than be alone, she set off through the forest to find him.

HERMIA: Lysander – what, removed? Lysander, lord!
What, out of hearing? Gone? No sound, no word?
Alack, where are you? Speak an if you hear.
Speak, of all loves! I swoon almost with fear.

ACT 3

Bottom, Peter Quince and the others were rehearsing[1] their play.

Bottom was to be Pyramus. In the play, Pyramus kills himself. Everyone was worried that the ladies in the audience would not like the killing. Bottom said that they should explain before the play began that he was Bottom, the weaver, and would not really die.

Snout thought that the ladies might be afraid of the lion. They decided to explain that the lion was really Snug, the joiner, and not a lion at all.

Puck saw them practising. He knew that Titania was sleeping very close by. He stayed to watch. Perhaps he could make some mischief.

Bottom made a speech as Pyramus. He went into some bushes to wait for his next turn. Puck followed Bottom into the bushes.

[1] rehearsing - practising

PUCK: A stranger Pyramus than e'er played here.
FLUTE: Must I speak now?
QUINCE: Ay, marry must you; for you must understand he goes but to see a noise that he heard, and is to come again.

Bottom came out of the bushes. He had only been in there a moment. Puck had given him a donkey's head. Bottom did not know there was anything wrong. He spoke his lines. He snorted like a donkey.

The others were terrified. What had happened to Bottom? They ran away. Puck was enjoying himself. He would lead them all over the forest.

BOTTOM: (as Pyramus)
- If I were fair, fair Thisbe, I were only thine.
QUINCE: O monstrous! O strange! We are haunted! Pray, masters!
Fly, masters! Help!

Bottom, left alone, sang a song to cheer himself up. His singing woke Titania. Oberon had put the magic juice on her eyes. Bottom with his ass's head was the first thing that she saw. She fell madly in love with Bottom.

TITANIA: I pray thee, gentle mortal, sing again!
Mine ear is much enamoured of thy note.
So is mine eye enthrallèd to thy shape,
And thy fair virtue's force perforce doth move me
On the first view to say, to swear, I love thee.

Titania was in love with Bottom. She told her fairies, Peaseblossom, Cobweb, Moth and Mustardseed to look after Bottom and make him happy. She told them to bring him wonderful fruits, to make candles to light his way to bed, and to fan him while he slept.

Bottom was very, very happy. He hadn't met fairies before. They called him "sir" and "master" and "your worship". When he spoke, he made snorting noises, like a donkey.

TITANIA: Be kind and courteous to this gentleman.
Hop in his walks and gambol in his eyes;
Feed him with apricocks and dewberries,
With purple grapes, green figs, and mulberries.

Puck met Oberon in the forest. He told Oberon that Titania was in love with an ordinary tradesman, who was wearing an ass's head. Puck had led the other tradesmen all through the forest.

Oberon was very pleased. Titania was in love with an ass. This was even better than he had hoped.

Just at that moment, Demetrius and Hermia came along.

PUCK: When in that moment – so it came to pass –
Titania waked, and straightway loved an ass.
OBERON: This falls out better than I could devise!

Hermia was still looking for Lysander. She didn't know that Puck had put the magic juice on Lysander's eyes. She didn't know that he had fallen in love with Helena. Hermia knew that Demetrius loved her, but she wanted Lysander. She could not understand why Lysander had gone away from her. She thought Demetrius might have killed him. She told Demetrius to leave her alone. She was going to look for Lysander. She was afraid he was dead.

Demetrius was very tired. He lay down and went to sleep.

Oberon realised that Puck had put the juice on the wrong man. Oberon's plan was to make Demetrius love Helena. He put the love juice on Demetrius's eyes. He told Puck to go and find Helena. Demetrius would wake and love her.

OBERON: Flower of this purple dye,
Hit with Cupid's archery,
Sink in apple of his eye.

Puck came back with Helena and Lysander. Helena still could not understand why Lysander had suddenly fallen in love with her.

At that moment, Demetrius awoke. Oberon had put the love juice on his eyes. He looked at Helena, and forgot his love for Hermia. He too loved Helena now.

Helena became very angry. She thought that Demetrius and Lysander were making fun of her.

DEMETRIUS: O, let me kiss
This princess of pure white, this seal of bliss!
HELENA: O spite! O hell! I see you all are bent
To set against me for your merriment.
If you were civil and knew courtesy
You would not do me thus much injury.

Hermia came looking for Lysander. He told her that he was in love with Helena.

Helena thought that all three of them had planned this as a cruel joke. She thought they were all acting.

Hermia and Helena had been friends since they were very young. They were like sisters. It made Helena even more angry to think that Hermia was part of the plan. She was sure that Hermia had helped to plan it as a joke.

Hermia could not believe that Lysander didn't love her any more. She clung to him, trying to change his mind.

LYSANDER: Hang off, thou cat, thou burr! Vile thing, let loose,
Or I will shake thee from me like a serpent.

HERMIA: Why are you grown so rude? What change is this,
Sweet love?

LYSANDER: Thy love? – out, tawny Tartar, out;
Out, loathed medicine! O hated potion, hence!

Once again, Hermia asked Lysander how he could have changed so quickly. She became angry with Helena. Helena had stolen Lysander's love.

Helena was taller than Hermia. Perhaps Lysander loved Helena because she was tall. Hermia wanted to scratch Helena's eyes out.

Demetrius and Lysander went to fight a duel[1]. They both loved Helena. Only one of them could marry her.

Helena was terrified of Hermia. She ran away, and Hermia ran after.

[1] duel - a fight to decide a quarrel

HERMIA: And are you grown so high in his esteem
Because I am so dwarfish and so low?
How low am I, thou painted maypole? Speak!
How low am I? – I am not yet so low
But that my nails can reach unto thine eyes.

Oberon and Puck saw Lysander and Demetrius fighting over Helena. Puck knew that he had made a mistake with Lysander, but he was enjoying all the trouble he had caused.

Oberon was worried because Demetrius and Lysander were going to fight a duel. Someone might get killed.

He told Puck to lead them through the forest, keeping them apart. Puck could imitate Lysander's voice, so that Demetrius would follow.

Oberon gave Puck a different magic juice. This was to take away the effect of the first one, the love juice. When Lysander fell down, tired, Puck was to squeeze it on Lysander's eyes. When Lysander awoke, he would love Hermia as he did before.

Oberon planned to use the same juice on Titania's eyes. She would forget her love for Bottom.

The sun would soon be coming up. The night was almost over.

LYSANDER: Where art thou, proud Demetrius? Speak thou now.
PUCK: (in Demetrius's voice):
Here, villain, drawn and ready! Where art thou?
LYSANDER: I will be with thee straight.
PUCK: (in Demetrius's voice)
Follow me then To plainer ground.

Puck led Lysander, then Demetrius, to a clear place in the forest. They fell asleep, tired out.

Helena, then Hermia, came along and also fell asleep.

Puck squeezed the "forgetting" juice onto Lysander's eyelids. When Lysander awoke, he would forget that he had been in love with Helena. He would be in love with Hermia again.

Demetrius would be in love with Helena. Everything would be as it should be.

PUCK: On the ground
Sleep sound.
I'll apply
To your eye,
Gentle lover, remedy.

ACT 4

Titania and the fairies looked after Bottom. He had a wonderful time. He and Titania were fast asleep.

Oberon was happy. At last, Titania had given him the Indian boy. It was time for her to stop loving Bottom. He dropped some juice on her eyelids.

Titania awoke. She couldn't believe that she had been in love with Bottom. She hated him now.

Puck took away the ass's head from Bottom. It was almost dawn. The fairies would have to hurry away.

Titania asked Oberon to tell her what had happened.

TITANIA: (wakes)
             My Oberon, what visions have I seen!
             Methought I was enamoured of an ass.
OBERON: There lies your love.
TITANIA: How came these things to pass?
              O, how mine eyes do loathe his visage now!

It was the morning of Theseus and Hippolyta's wedding day. They were hunting in the forest. Egeus, Hermia's father, was hunting with them.

They found Lysander, Demetrius, Helena and Hermia asleep on the ground.

The huntsmen sounded their horns to wake them.

Egeus was angry. Hermia had tried to run away.

Demetrius now loved Helena. He didn't want to marry Hermia any more.

Puck had used the "forgetting" juice on Lysander. Lysander loved Hermia again. There were now three happy couples, Theseus and Hippolyta, Hermia and Lysander, and Helena and Demetrius.

Theseus decided there would be no hunting that day. The three couples would all be married together. They went to prepare for the wedding.

Later that day, Bottom returned to his friends. They were very happy to see him. They could put on their play for Duke Theseus.

EGEUS: My lord, this is my daughter here asleep,
And this Lysander; this Demetrius is,
This Helena - old Nedar's Helena.
I wonder of their being here together.

ACT 5

Theseus and Hippolyta, Helena and Demetrius, Hermia and Lysander were married. It was the evening of their wedding day. They were all very happy.

Theseus decided they would watch the tradesmen's play of Pyramus and Thisbe.

Peter Quince read his prologue[1]. He was so nervous that he stopped in all the wrong places. His prologue didn't really make sense. The nobles thought it was quite funny. They interrupted, and made loud comments.

---

[1] prologue - a speech at the beginning of a play, explaining what the play is to be about

QUINCE: All for your delight
We are not here. That you should here repent you
The actors are at hand, and by their show
You shall know all that you are like to know.

THESEUS: This fellow does not stand upon points.

LYSANDER: He hath rid his prologue like a rough colt; he knows not the stop.

Snout was the Wall in the play. He held out his fingers to make the hole in the Wall.

Pyramus, played by Bottom, and Thisbe, played by Flute, were supposed to whisper and kiss through the hole in the wall.

BOTTOM: (as Pyramus)
O, kiss me through the hole of this vile wall.
FLUTE: (as Thisbe)
I kiss the wall's hole, not your lips at all.

Snug, who took the part of the Lion, told the ladies not to be afraid. He was not a real lion, but only Snug, the joiner.

Starveling was Moonshine. He explained that he was the man in the moon, with a lantern, a bush, and a dog.

Pyramus and Thisbe were to meet by moonlight. The lion frightened Thisbe away.

Pyramus thought the lion had killed Thisbe. He killed himself.

Finding her lover dead, Thisbe killed herself.

After this sad ending, the players did a dance.

BOTTOM: Will it please you to see the epilogue, or to hear a Bergomask dance between two of our company?

Everyone had enjoyed the comedy of *Pyramus and Thisbe*. The wedding day was over.

Oberon and Titania were happily together again. With their fairies, they came to bless the three couples who had been married that day.

While everyone slept, they went through the palace. Their magic would bring good luck.

Puck said good night to everyone. He said the story might have been a dream – a Midsummer Night's Dream?

PUCK: If we shadows have offended,
Think but this, and all is mended:
That you have but slumbered here
While these shadows did appear.